and God wants People

by Mary Lou Lacy

and God
wants People

JOHN KNOX PRESS
RICHMOND, VIRGINIA

Some of the ideas developed in this book were included in two articles by Mary Lou Lacy published in *Concern,* the official magazine of United Presbyterian Women, November 1959 and May 1960, and are used here by permission.

The quotations from James 3:7-10 and Matthew 25:34-40 are from The New English Bible (New Testament), published 1961 by Oxford University Press and Cambridge University Press. John 17:12 is from the Revised Standard Version. Other quoted Scripture is from the King James Version.

To six special blessings
—my sisters and brother

Contents

because $\mathcal{G}od$ *loves*

$\mathcal{N}$EXT TO GOD, OTHER PEOPLE are all in this world that matter! How do I know? The very same way you'll know if you think about God, and yourself, and the only possible result of this relationship.

Surely, if more than one man had not been so essential, God would have stopped with Adam. In one sense, no more was needed to complete Creation. There was God, and His child, and a wonderful, beautiful world. There was God's love for man and man's capacity to love Him in return. In the beginning, the two of them could walk together, commune with each other, enjoy a common friendship that required no lofty cathedral other than His earth and sky. Was this not completeness? Why, then, should God take a chance on spoiling it all? For what purpose did He add complications—other people?

In another sense, the sense of God's infinite wisdom, just one man wasn't enough—not enough for God Himself, not even enough for Adam. Why? Think it through in your own relationship with God. He has done everything to express His love for you. You cannot even name all the ways He has said, "You are my child, and I love you. Because I love you, I have done this for you, and made this for you, and will continue to provide this for you. And this, and this, for you—." You can never count all the ways God proves how He feels about you. And here we are, you and I, receiving, accepting, demanding, with no way in this world of offering proof to God that we love Him back in return; with no way, save one. Mere man can never express his feelings toward God except through his relationship with other people.

We cannot say, "God, we truly love You, and because of it we will do this and this for You, Yourself." Actually, there is nothing we can do for God; He needs nothing from us except a response of love for Him that envelops other people. That's how we react to what He means to us, and it's the only way we can offer Him service, or gifts, or pure honest-to-goodness love. This love for others cannot be separated from man's feelings toward his Heavenly Father. Maybe you can love people without loving God, but you cannot love God without caring deeply, sincerely, yearningly about other human beings.

Think a little more. What does God want from man? Obedience? Why, yes, He requires that, but He wants it as a response to His overflowing feeling toward His child. He wants obedience springing from a uniting of their desires, His and man's; obedience resulting from a common purpose, a oneness of spirit. Of course He wants man's adoration, his worship, his loftiest love, but He wants these to bear results that can only be accomplished on and toward other people.

Perhaps if we look at the Ten Commandments we can understand more clearly. When God told Moses to set down in definite words what He expected of man, He did not say merely, "Love me, obey me, trust me, worship me." No. He said, "If you take these first four rules that I give you, then there are six more that will have to follow. Your only response to a relationship with me is reflected in your regard for your fellow men." Jesus said the same thing, didn't He? The first and greatest commandment is "Love God," then the second necessarily comes, "and your neighbor as yourself."

So, you see, if you and I truly believe God, as He gives the beginning pattern of love, if we truly believe Jesus, as He straightens men out again, then we have no choice but to believe that next to God, other people are all in this world that matter.

Maybe you cannot accept this altogether just yet. Maybe you'd like to think about it awhile and awhile.

Perhaps you have this reaction to the idea: "If this author-person is right, if all my feelings toward God are reflected in my dealings with my fellow men, then why am I at odds with them so much of the time? Why can't I show this love I feel for God so that I always say the right thing, do the kind deed? Why can't I feel successful in my relationships instead of continuously being misunderstood, or forever not knowing how to express what God means to me?"

Well, if you—and I—admit that we fall far short in our dealings with each other, if we honestly confess that here is where we have the most difficult assignment, if we finally understand that all Christ asks in proof of our love for Him is that we care for His children, feed His sheep, then the time has come to make a new beginning. I must start afresh. Must you? Perhaps if we attempt this new realization together, we can strengthen each other. Let's think it through, let's seek it out, let's give God a chance to stretch our comprehension. Will you begin with me what we might call an experiment in human understanding? When we attempt it together, who knows, it just might happen that the three of us—God, and you, and I—will grow very close indeed!

CHAPTER 1

God's most Difficult Task

"Let not your heart be troubled: ye believe in God, believe also in me" (John 14:1).

I WISH THAT we didn't invariably associate these words with death. You cannot blame a minister for turning straight to this passage when he faces the family and friends of a person whose soul has left the body and whose life, as we see it, has ended. There is great comfort in knowing that Jesus and our loved ones are united in the spacious house of Heaven. It helps to be told that rooms will be made ready there for us too. This is blessed assurance to our aching, terror-filled hearts as we say to ourselves, "There, now, don't be so afraid of death. Don't feel that this person you love has ceased to be. He is somewhere with

God, in the life beyond, and you can count on that happening to you when you die." Jesus' words referred to the separation that His death would bring and were meant to bring comfort to His disciples.

But doesn't this picture of our Lord offer another comfort too —companionship in life? For here is Jesus pouring out His heart, saying over and over again to His friends, "Oh, I love you. I care so much about you. There will never be a time when I don't yearn for you. And, through my Spirit, I'll always stay with you, every minute of the day, every second of the night. You can count on this. Though everything else in life changes, this, my love for you, is yours eternally. So, my beloved (and this is the glorious thing we miss at funerals, at deathbeds, at sorrow-filled meditations), don't be afraid to live. You are with God now. You have the assurance of His Presence now. You have something to live for, and with, and on *now*—my all-encompassing love."

Do you see what I mean? If you do not, try reading the Gospel of John, chapters thirteen through sixteen, at a time when the sorrows of life, not death, are pressing down upon your heart. Read these chapters then, and see if you don't get the ultimate picture of how much Jesus loves you. He tries in every way possible to make you understand. He kneels down, He washes feet —everyone's feet, even those that immediately rush out to betray Him. And then He begins to speak. I can see Him sitting there, leaning forward earnestly, pleadingly, beseechingly, toward those eleven men who represent you and me. He calls them "Little children," a term that makes me think of a father talking to his tiny child, "Oh, my sweet, precious little baby." Complete self-giving, complete acceptance of ownership, complete realization of the child's dependence on him!

Our Savior looks yearningly from one disciple to the other throughout His discourse, as over and over He declares, "I love you. I care about you. Oh, please, understand that no matter what, you can depend on my loving you."

Have you ever tried to make someone know how much you cared about him and felt that he didn't understand at all? You try to tell him in words, in little self-humbling acts, in overlooking his apparent lack of love for you, and finally, in just keeping on loving him, no matter what. That's the way Jesus does. We know it because of what happened to Peter. But it's so hard for us to believe it about ourselves.

Therefore, I have decided that God's most difficult task is to make us know that He loves us.

"Wait," you say, "surely the Cross was His hardest ordeal! The redemptive payment of a crucified body—without a doubt this was God's most costly act!"

I don't think that even this supreme suffering was as hard for God as making us know that it was done for us. The act of redemption is accomplished; the burden of making us believe, and accept, and use the love involved, still is borne by God.

It seems almost sacrilegious to say you feel sorry for Jesus. But if you truly try to place yourself in His company that last night of being with His closest friends, your heart almost breaks for Him (as His does for you). You see how hard He tries to crowd into those few remaining minutes of fellowship the whole essence of His Being—His love for His children, His disciples, you, me.

I remember, once, when I was in the hospital after a major operation, I thought that I was about to die. None of the people dearest to me happened to be there at the time, and I felt the great urgency of leaving messages for each of them. Strangely enough, I wasn't too concerned about what would happen to my few possessions, or who would take care of my children, or the grief that my death would cause my family. There was only one thing I wanted to set straight with all of my dearest ones. I found myself saying over and over to the nurse, "Tell them that I love them." Then I repeated, "Tell this one and that one that I have truly cared about them. Tell him that my love for him has been a precious thing to me. Oh, tell each of them that I love them!"

Nothing else seemed to matter to me then. I was willing to spend my last breath getting this across. A little later, when I was much better, the nurse and I joked about my messages. To her it was a laughing matter. She knew all along that I was not going to die, but I didn't know it. To this day I like to remember what means the most when you think life is over.

Jesus knew that He was going to die. He knew that only a few minutes were left to Him to say the things dearest to His heart. He did not use this precious time to set up a plan for expansion of His church. He didn't delegate duties to this disciple or that one. He just tried, with all His heart, to make them know that He loved them, and that, in response to this love, a way of life would open up to them. Now, mind you, I said, "a way of life," not death.

And then Jesus gave His friends a promise. He told them that even though He, in His present form, would have to go away, He would never leave them without the comfort of His Presence. He said, "The Spirit of God will live in you. This is my Spirit. He will feed you, nourish you, guide you, counsel you, as you let Him take command. Always be aware of this Spirit, for He is the part of you that is a living part of me, just like the vine and the branches." Could anything be more indicative of His feeling for us than this gift and His other one—the Cross?

So, "let not your heart be troubled." Cast "all your care upon him; for he careth for you." Words to live by! How much I need this assurance! Maybe you don't. Maybe you seldom have times of loneliness, or failure, or utter desperation, but if you do, perhaps there are steps we can take to make God's task with us less difficult.

Because you and I both need to be sure, continuously, that God loves us, let us embark upon the first step of our experiment together. Let's admit that we are not fully aware of how much God wants us. Let's try to find definite ways to open up our minds and hearts to a day-by-day, minute-by-minute, second-by-second consciousness of His love. We haven't anything to lose! And, oh, how much we have to gain!

EXPERIMENT—Stage One

Objective: To know beyond all doubt that God loves us beyond measure.

Beginning right now we will look around us for evidences of God's love. When we see a robin wing its way to a limb outside our window let us say:

> A bird, a tree, a bright sunny day,
> All gifts my eyes can see.
> My heart sings out, "This is the way
> God shows His love to me."

Just practice, practice, determinedly practice looking for evidence of God's caring. You'll see it in events that take place, in sudden results of haphazard planning, in unexpected blessings of the day. You'll even recognize it in the way your mind moves from one thought to another; the unconscious humming of a song; the sudden companionship of prayer; and you just might be able to see it in people who come your way.

Wake up in the morning declaring, "God loves me. I am not alone for one single minute." Fall asleep at night whispering, "His Spirit is within me. He loves me, no matter what." And, all in between, be conscious, conscious, conscious that Jesus is leaning forward toward you, His disciple, saying, "Don't be afraid. Don't be troubled. Remember, I offer you a love to live by. Take it, my child, accept it."

the Lesson of the Clock

CAN WE KNOW, with a great deal more assurance now, that God's love for us is ever-present, is surrounding each aspect of our existence, is so completely offered to us in Jesus Christ that we will never wander outside the realm of His caring? If we can, the experiment has begun to work.

But let us be ever so careful not to stop here. Keep thinking, "God loves me," a thousand times a day, but don't believe for one single minute that this will be the end of it. It's just the beginning!

I'd like to share with you a lesson that my father taught us

many years ago. I wish you and everyone could have known him.
His delightful sense of humor, his amazing ability to perceive
how people felt inside, his complete disinterest in his own personal possessions, made him the most surprising, wonderful,
stimulating person you ever met. Sometimes he quite took your
breath away with his unpredictable actions, such as the day that
he traded two automobiles at once, his and the one parked behind it. The second one belonged to an out-of-town yarn salesman who had just happened to drop by on business that morning. Even now the salesman declares that this was the best trade-
in deal he ever made. But you can imagine his surprise as he
drove home in a new car that night. Once you knew my father
you got used to surprises.

There were seven children in our family. Every year, as we
approached the Christmas season, we would give much thought
to finding the right gift for Daddy. He was always our biggest
problem. There was simply nothing that he needed. You have at
least one name like that on your list, haven't you? Well, our
father had no particular hobbies so we couldn't give him hunt-
ing or fishing equipment or golf balls. He bought whatever
clothes he needed, as he needed them, quite often two suits
just alike. "Why not?" he would say. "If one is right for you,
why not two?" And, with the same philosophy of choice, he
would buy a dozen ties, handkerchiefs, and pairs of socks. He
wouldn't keep his money in a wallet, but distributed it around
in many pockets so that he could reach in and bring out, to the
penny, just the amount you asked for. With seven children this
was a wise procedure. We were never quite sure that we had
not taken his last cent. Sometimes we could get him a new hat,
but there was always the possibility that he would give it away
to the first bareheaded man he met. You can understand, can't
you, why Daddy was a problem at Christmas?

Every year we would beg him to tell us something he wanted,

and every year he would give us no satisfaction at all. That is, every year but one. On this particular occasion, he secretly confessed to me that there was an item he really and truly needed. He offered to impart this information to me under certain provisions. First, he asked me to promise that I would not let anyone else know that he had confided in me. I promised! Next, he asked me to give my solemn vow that I would tell no one what my gift to him would be. I gave that solemn vow! Then, he asked my word that I would pay only a minimum amount for the object he would request. My word came forthwith! Finally, being very sure that no one else was around, he told me that he wanted a clock. He'd like a small clock for his mantel or his bedside table.

Smugly, I approached the Yuletide. None of the old nagging uncertainties of what to get Daddy shadowed my happiness. Not only was my problem taken care of, but a deeper joy was mine. I, I was the favored one. Out of seven children asking, he had decided to answer me. I was his choice, his special person, his one-to-love-the-most child! I even felt a little pity for my sisters and brother who knew not the glow of being a favorite of their father. "Oh, well," I thought, "it's only natural that, with so many children, he would have to love one the most."

Do you know what happened on Christmas morning? We gathered to open our gifts, and, as usual, my father was the last to begin on his. He had the undivided attention of the group. In order to enjoy my triumphant feeling to the fullest, I managed a seat quite close to his as he started on his first package. And I sat there, as if glued to my chair, watching him open and arrange, in a neat straight line, SEVEN—I counted them—SEVEN little clocks. With the greatest of glee, he had told each one of his children the same secret!

At first, my feelings were hurt. I couldn't understand why he would do this thing, why he would play such a dreadful, horrible joke on me, on all of us. And then it began to sink in. He never said it in words—that wasn't his method—but he had found a way that we'd never forget to say to us, his seven children, "I love you all. I love each of you very much. But loving one more than another is not the way my father-heart beats. Know, within yourself, that you are a very special person to me, but also know that my other children are just as dear, just as important as you. And perhaps, because you are so close to me, you will draw closer to each other."

Does that lesson of the clocks help you any? It does me. Here I am, brushing up against people every day, liking some of them so much, disliking others just as vehemently, having to work out a relationship with each one, expecting each to be different from what he is, wishing she would change this part of her nature, upset because he responds so differently from the way I think he should. Here I am, having all of these feelings about other people, with no end to my frustrations until I suddenly realize: "God made them and loves them just as He does me. He yearns after them and uses them just as He works in and through me. To each of them He speaks just as surely as He reveals Himself to me. And it's this same Holy Spirit in all that makes us close, close kin, members of the household of God."

Don't you see that it is just as important that we have a continuous certainty that God loves other people as it is to be sure that He cares about us? Honestly now, isn't this the basic fact that could make all the difference in the world in our relationships with each other?

Little irritations like having to stop for a car that pulls out in front of us in traffic would affect us so differently if we could stifle the "Who does he think he is?" reaction and simply answer the question: "He is someone God loves, and he is in an awful hurry."

And instead of feeling offended when someone we know passes us by without so much as a nod of recognition, we might be able to think: "Bless her heart! She does need glasses, but perhaps she is afraid they might make her look older than her husband." You see, we begin to try to understand when we reach the point of knowing that God cares about others just as He does about us.

How often we are warned against the sin of pride. What is pride? Well, really, it's some form of a "me-being-better-than-you" feeling. It couldn't exist unless there was a comparison idea in the back of our minds. I wonder what it would do to our pride if we began today to take note of all the ways God shows His love for other people. If you feel superior because of your looks (secretly, many people do), just take note of the physical blessings God has dealt to others. "What a lovely smile she has. God gave it. How broad and strong his shoulders. God formed them. What blue, blue eyes, what pretty hair, what beautiful hands. God made them all. How thankful they should be to Him—and so should I!"

If you take pride in your abilities, your accomplishments, your qualities of character, look around you at the God-given attributes of others and you'll soon be deciding: "To be gentle as she is, that's quite a gift. To be considerate as he is, ah, that's something of value." Kindness and unselfishness, honesty and patience, forgiveness and humility—these should be the cravings of the spirit of man, fruits of the Spirit of God. And we cannot observe these qualities in other people without knowing full well that God is in them, working and directing and blessing through their yielding to His will.

EXPERIMENT—Stage Two

Objective: To become certain that God loves others, too.

Take the lesson of the clock and "install" it in your mind and heart. The only things that we install are things that we have a definite use for, things that do a particular job for us. Well, use the idea that whomever you meet today is a favorite of his Father. He has been sought out for a special relationship with God. Oh, he might not know it, might never have been aware of his eternal value, but you know it. And this is where the crux of the matter lies. Because you know that God loves him you experience a kinship, a "member-of-the-same-family" feeling. Today, you will see clocks all around you. Notice the dials divided into minutes and seconds and remember that wherever they are placed on the face, the long hand and the short hand sweep them all. Think of God as the Long Hand continuously covering every tiny unit. Think of yourself as the short hand. As He includes you, you include His other children. The Long Hand of God, the short hand of His child—all-encompassing, all-inclusive! How differently we begin to look at other people!

CHAPTER 3

Not-Me, Lord!

"A new commandment I give unto you, That ye love one another; as I have loved you, that ye also love one another" (John 13:34).

"These things I command you, that ye love one another" (John 15:17).

HE SON OF GOD, the Ruler of all nature, the Beginning and the End, the Savior of the World, never demanded that men who love Him do but one other thing: love one another. It is vital to understand that He did not make this a request, or a hopeful wish, or an optional suggestion. He made it a command, a no-alternative order. Not "try to love each other," or "do the best you can to love each other," or "it will please me greatly if you love one another." On the contrary, He just demands it, and He leaves no doubt about the caliber of the love He requires. He simply adds the qualifying clause, "as I have loved you." "You must grow my kind of love," He says.

Oh, dear! That makes all the difference, doesn't it? The kind of love that Jesus lived was the kneeling-down, feet-washing, life-giving, dying-on-the-cross love. And here He is telling you and me, His disciples, in no uncertain terms, that He expects love like this from us. There is no other interpretation of these clear-cut directives. If you think you can find a way to twist their meaning into something else, read again those chapters in John (thirteen through sixteen) and you'll have to admit that it's as plain as the nose on your face.

"If I really make a difference to you," He says, "then it will show in the way you feel toward other people. As your response to my love for you, I command you to love each other."

This isn't the only time or place that He makes such a requirement, is it? "Do you love me?" He asks Peter, and you, and me. This is after He has hung on the cross, paying for Peter's sins, and yours, and mine. "Do you love me? Well, prove it. Prove it in the only way you can. Translate your feelings for me into an active caring for my other children. It will not be difficult to love some of these. Feed my little lambs."

These we can feed with pleasure and a feeling of success. Helpless, weak, lovable, precious little lambs that call out the best from our hearts, these inspire a ready response. "Oh, yes," we hasten to agree. "Yes, Lord, we will care for your little lambs; they are attractive, easy-to-feed children of Thine."

But what about the sheep? What about the ugly, smelly, disagreeable, unappreciative, stubborn, resentful, dirty old sheep? Ah, there's a different story. "Feed my sheep," Jesus insisted. "Love the unlovely. Don't let the way they look on the outside make a difference to you, for I know what they are like on the inside, and I love them. Therefore, you must too. So feed all to whom I am the Good Shepherd. This is what I require of you."

It might be important right here, lest you and I become too discouraged to continue the Experiment, that we understand what He means by "love." Whenever we say to ourselves, "I just cannot love that person; if Jesus expects that of me, well, it's more than impossible," then perhaps we are misinterpreting what Jesus means. Do you think He taught that the Good Samaritan was required to enjoy forever the company of the man he helped on the Jericho road? Did He ever give the impression that He, Himself, would find equal delight in an evening of fellowship with every person He met? But can't we be sure that He found special pleasure in the happy home of Mary and Martha?

Jesus never said, "Enjoy all men." Instead He said, "Feel toward all men a compassion, a kindliness, a regard, a responsibility, a 'love' that will make you reach out immediately to help them in any way you can." So, when He said to Peter, and to us, "Feed my sheep," He said quite plainly, "There are always things you can do for other people to let them know that you recognize them as my children, your brothers, whom you care about because you know that they belong to me. This is what I require of you. This is my new commandment to you. It's new because, until now, no one ever gladly accepted the burdens of other people; no one ever saw in all men enough goodness to make them worth dying for. I see this worth, and because I show you this new way, you can see this dignity of man too."

A father found it very difficult to tell his little girl, Jane, a new story every night. He did not have the kind of imagination to invent new characters or exciting adventures. So he did the best he could and made each story about Jane, her friends, her toys, her family. This type of entertainment did not appeal to the little girl. "No, Daddy," she would protest as he began his once-upon-a-time-there-was-a-little-girl-named-Jane. "No, don't tell about Jane. Tell about not-Jane." So the father would begin again, "Once upon a time, there was a little girl named Not-Jane. And Not-Jane had a doll called Not-Susie. One day Not-Jane took Not-Susie over to visit her friend Not-Mary." Then the story would continue to the child's perfect satisfaction. She did not want to look objectively at herself. She disliked the feeling that the bad things the little girl in the story did were her own faults. She could disapprove with scorn Not-Jane's habit of leaving her toys scattered about. She could laugh with derision when Not-Jane dropped her selfishly obtained biggest piece of cake into the mud. She could even find real satisfaction in hearing that Not-Jane's mother made her sit in a chair for an hour after she threw sand in Not-Mary's hair.

Now, who does this remind you of? "No one," we say, until we become perfectly honest. It's all right for Jesus to look old Peter straight in the eye and say, "Make me believe it, Peter. Make me certain that you'll take my new commandment seriously. There's nothing you can do for me except love all of these people. Love them, Peter, in a way that requires definite action." But, to us, Peter is a Not-Jane character, a not-us person, and we had rather not feel the eyes of our Master turned toward us, compelling us to look back at Him. We had rather not hear the words, "You are the one to whom I give this command. You are the one who has failed to respond to human need all about you. You are the one who has never felt the responsibility that comes with loving me. You are the one who has accepted my caring for you. You have seen me hanging upon the cross in payment for your sins. So, now, you must love me in a new way, my way. Feed my lambs, even feed my sheep. This is what I require of you."

Oh, not-me, Lord, not-me! Tell this to anyone else and it makes sense; it seems easy. But don't measure me, Lord, not-me!

EXPERIMENT—Stage Three

Objective: To understand that loving others is the only proof of our love for Him.

Let's try to make today's part of the Experiment as simple as possible. Let's not set too high a goal, such as trying to look at everyone in the light of the new command. We'd either fail completely and give up, or we'd put mankind into a big nameless "lump" and develop the "God-bless-everybody" attitude that we learned, as children, would shorten our prayers.

Let's concentrate on just three people. Pick them out carefully, prayerfully. The first is someone you love very much. The second is someone you dislike equally as much. Oh, how you do dislike him! The third is a person whom you have just met, so you have no particular attitude at all about this one. Pick them out honestly, earnestly, after you have asked God's guidance along the way.

All right, starting with the one you love, try to decide what it is about him, or her, that deserves the sacrifice of a Savior hanging on the cross. You will find nothing that justifies such a caring, but you will find many qualities that show evidence of this person's belonging to a God who cares. Try it.

Next, name the admirable traits of the one you dislike. You might need a pencil and paper with this one. You might have to tell yourself, "I will not give up until I accomplish this assignment. I will keep trying until I find something good to write down." You'll take longer discovering the first quality than you will the second, so, just to play fairly, make yourself list two. Nothing here to deserve Eternal Life! But there are two, or three, or maybe more good things that you never recognized before. "Suppose I find none," you ask, "what then?" Perhaps it will be well for us to think a long, long time before we decide that we are wiser than God, that a person, shaped in His image, by His own hand, has no reason for being!

Take the person you have just met. What a challenge to find out why God made him, why Jesus cares!

CHAPTER 4

Hooks and Scars

and Hidden Cars

THOUGH YOU SPEAK with tongues of men and of angels and have not human understanding, you are a noisy gong or a clanging cymbal. And though you can explain the Scriptures in a learned fashion and quote from the latest commentaries with complete assurance, even if you master the art of holding twelve-year-old boys spellbound as you expound the Minor Prophets, and still have not human understanding, you are nothing. If you put every penny (and dollar, too) into the offering plate each Sunday morning, if you work in the church kitchen every time there is a supper, if you learn to call all members of your congregation by their first names, yea, even if you come into the House of God each time its doors are opened, and have not human understanding, you gain nothing.

Understanding is patient, kind, not jealous of another's good fortune, not self-exalting, or rude. Understanding does not insist on its own way, is not irritable, or resentful. It is touched by sadness when someone else has unhappiness, and finds great delight in another's good fortune. Human understanding is able to take whatever happens, always believing the best of people. Human understanding never, never gives up in reaching out with compassion.

Why substitute for the word love? Because we have used that wonderful word so cheaply, so commonly, that we very rarely consider it in its original meaning. Why, just the other day, I noticed a sign attached to the back of a taxi. In large letters was the word "LOVE." "Good," I thought, "the cab drivers are promoting brotherly love. They are reminding us all of our reason for being." But as I came closer and was able to adjust my eyes to the smaller print, this is what screamed out at me from that sign: "Love at the first Bite! Try Hastleberry's Chili Sauce. You'll Love it!"

What have we done to the holiness of that blessed, vital word? And what have we done to ourselves in putting the original intent of that word out of practice? Oh, how shamefully we fail, simply by not taking the command of Christ seriously enough, by not reaching out in love, actually, wholeheartedly, unfailingly!

By now, you and I should have come to the conclusion that no matter what happens to society, whatever government, economic, or social structure changes we endure, this fact never alters: next to God, other people are all in this world that matter. Of course, if one does not truly believe in God, if one does not know that His redemptive love is a vital necessity, if one feels that to face life he needs nothing beyond himself, then, well, then other people don't really matter at all. But be sure—be very sure —that you can do without God before you decide that a single person you meet is worthless, or trivial, or unimportant.

Perhaps you don't ever listen to the radio, now that television has moved in. It is only when I travel many miles in my automobile that I tune in to the station nearest my route. Riding all day in the company of a car radio I find myself giving the latest news every hour on the hour right along with the announcer. I learn the silliest jingles whether I want to or not, and without knowing it, I begin to advertise bottled drinks, toothpaste, and patent medicines as I absently hum a catchy tune. But the greatest asset to my education are the hit tunes that I come to recognize from the first few doo-wa doo-wa be-bo be-dos of the background music. My greatest difficulty, however, is to get these important contributions to modern music out of my head once they get a footing. Not long ago a noisy jangle, called "Charlie Brown," stuck itself in my mind, and I found that my heart would not let it go.

In the midst of the clanging bedlam the music stops, and a pitifully pathetic voice says, "Why is everybody always picking on me?" Poor Charlie Brown! He feels desperately sure that no one understands him, or loves him. No matter how hard I try to forget him I have become painfully conscious of the many "Charlie Browns" I meet each day. I even recognize the dark days when I, myself, am a "Charlie Brown," feeling completely out of tune with the people I brush up against.

Now why is it that we, who claim to love God with all our hearts, have such a hard time completing the command? Why do we find such difficulty in getting along with other people? Do you suppose it could be that we count on this relationship just springing up, perfect, without any striving on our part? And then, when there isn't this spontaneous delight in each other, we decide that understanding is an impossibility. That's not true.

God intended us to be happy, and understanding each other is essential to happiness.

Strangely enough, we are just waking up to the fact that getting along with people does not necessarily come naturally. In the last ten or fifteen years, there has been a sudden realization on the part of business, industry, government, and religion that human relations is a field we have neglected far too long, that it should be emphasized, studied, worked at, in order for us to live happily side by side.

Twice each year, a very large furniture factory nearby brings in a prominent Southern minister who has put his full-time energies into a God-centered approach toward the art of understanding. He travels from one industry to another, teaching the sales forces, the office personnel, the plant workers, that good human relations is vital in business, and that we must work at getting along with people. Industry feels that such a consideration is a necessity because it pays off in dollars and cents.

The church has suddenly become aware that the most effective Christianity is that which is able to reach out and begin where a person is in understanding. In almost every denomination you'll find that seminaries have recently begun new departments of Human Relations, Counseling, Personal Understanding.

Not any more do we assume that just because two people speak the same language, live on the same street, go to the same church, they necessarily understand each other. Take you and me, for instance. We had completely different beginnings, different family traits, different physical characteristics, different experiences, so how is it possible for me to know exactly how you feel and think and hope just from the way I do? I cannot, and, because you act differently from the way I would act, you are strange; you are hard to get along with; you are misunderstood by me.

My favorite illustration, one used by a counseling expert, tells of a school of happy little fish swimming along together, having whatever communication little fish have with each other. Suddenly, one little fish begins to turn, and twist, and splash, and sputter. The other little fish notice and say, "What's with him? Why doesn't he behave like little fish are supposed to behave? Who is he trying to impress?" Then, swoosh, and the strange little fish is gone. What his brothers did not know was that, on the bank, there was a man who had a pole, a line, and a hook. The strange little fish had a hook in him!

Poor Charlie Brown! "Why is everybody always picking on me?" He probably has a hook in him that we know nothing about. And so do I, some days, and so do you. And so does the man or the woman who acts so strangely that we give up and leave him or her alone. Hooks are hard to identify, hard to recognize, but once you and I truly want to grow in human understanding, we will be able to look beyond the hook and find something worth while in every person that God has made. And we won't have to know the circumstances, we'll merely have to care!

One cold Sunday morning, when the radiators in our crowded kindergarten department were hissing out the steam, I met little Doug at the door to help him take off his coat. As I tried to unzip without catching his chin, he planted both hands squarely on his chest. "No," he said. "Come on, Doug," I pleaded, "the other children have their coats off." "No." "It's hot in here, and you'll catch cold when you go outside." "No."

It took two adults to remove one small boy's jacket, but victory was ours at last, and the coat hung in the closet while Doug hung unhappily on the outside of the group activities. When his mother came at the end of the period, I confessed that, for the first time, I had trouble with Doug. "Just couldn't make him take off his coat," I said. How do you suppose I felt when the mother explained? "You see, it's a new coat," she whispered, "the very first new coat Doug has ever owned. All the rest have been hand-me-downs from his older brother." And then trying to excuse myself, I said the unpardonable thing for a Christian: "I wish I had known; I would have acted differently." Seeing only the external needs of that little boy I had failed completely in human understanding.

It is interesting to me how words suddenly take on new meanings and become associated with new ideas. "Tars" is one that almost instantly hit the public eye. "Hidden tars" are proclaimed as enemies of the smoking population. They lurk dangerously somewhere within the confines of the cigarette between the "up-front" section and the other end. They cannot be eliminated or dealt with before the product is made. They must be recognized as an embedded sin that can be filtered away through the cleverness of the manufacturer.

"Hidden tars" seem to be what people have deep inside of them. These qualities, which we'd rather not have and would gladly purge away if we could, are embedded within the makings of us all. It is only through the cleansing, changing, regenerating power of the Spirit of God that these "tars" can be filtered out and rendered helpless to destroy us. Every person we meet has these enemies within him just the same as we do, and to love him we must recognize that his filter is the same as ours; his filter is God's Spirit, too.

> Hooks and scars and hidden tars
> Are things we cannot see
> That make a man the way he is,
> Not as he wants to be!

There is another problem in this business of getting along together. We become so preoccupied with the complexities of life that we often look past people, completely unaware that here is kinship needing to be claimed.

A friend who was in the Air Force during the last World War told of an airstrip being built with Chinese labor. Because there was very little modern machinery available, Chinese peasants were used to move huge rollers in order to level the dirt. As fifty or more men pulled, the flyer saw one stumble and fall. The workers did not stop to pick up their ailing brother but merely continued to roll the heavy machinery over his body as though it were not there. So little regard for human life, so little care for the man who worked beside them! It's horrible to think about, and yet, are not we Americans, who pretend to be so aware of individual rights, guilty of treating people as if they were not there?

We tend to look through others, forgetting that they feel, and hurt, and care, and want, and wish, and matter just as we ourselves, forgetting that every individual is a child of God and made in His image.

"Wait a minute, just one minute," you are probably thinking, as I would be too if I had not begun a little earlier than you in this whole embarrassing affair. "You're being too critical of me. I'm a Christian. Brotherly love is what I profess. Why, my friends all think I'm the best kind of person, so mindful of their feelings, so conscious of their needs. I'm perfectly aware of other people."

Are you? Can you truthfully say that you never fail in meeting human needs? Are you willing to bother with everyone you meet? What about the people you see each day? Do you reach out in understanding to everyone, those who sell you newspapers, sweep your office or your home, fill your tank with gas, serve you food, clean your clothes, wait on you in stores, walk along the street with you, sit at the end of your church pew? Or do you look through them as though they were not there? Steamroller tactics, such as too-busy schedules, keep us from offering understanding to people—people who matter most of all, next to God.

I knew a lady who had the capacity for love that made everyone, anyone, she came in contact with feel worthy. She gave them dignity simply by the way in which she showed respect for their worth as individuals. The boy who cut her grass became a person of importance as she thanked him and paid him not just with money but with appreciation. The clerk in the store would meet the next customer with new hope and greater determination to please because "Miss Annie" had made her feel that, in being a good clerk, she had much to offer the world. The friend who poured out her heartbreak would leave "Miss Annie's" presence knowing that always, always, God can use grief to enlarge the scope of the human heart. Why, she could even make Charlie Brown know that he was somebody! "Have you met my good friend, Mr. Charles Brown?" she would have said, making him feel like a most important person; "I'm sure you'll like him." That's the kind of lifting up "Miss Annie" did continuously, and with the frailest of shoulders.

Perhaps by now you are saying, "All right, suppose I do agree that we haven't really tried hard enough to obey the 'Neighbour as thyself' command. I'm willing to go halfway, but this other fellow, suppose he won't meet me there?" Well, we have only one answer to that: halfway is not enough.

When we were children, I used to walk halfway home with a friend who came to play. And she, in turn, would walk halfway back with me. Then I would go halfway again with her, neither one of us ending where we belonged. It was most frustrating, for, you see, halfway just wasn't enough. And it's not enough in human relations. So, where do we start? We start where the person is—exactly where the other person is. Don't expect him to be where you are, for you did not begin at the same place.

But you can find him wherever he is, because in your response to God's love, you realize how much he really matters.

Let us seek the path that Jesus makes in approaching other people. Remember Him at the well in Samaria. He did not start by criticizing that woman or by trying to change her immediately. No, He merely began where she was, at the well, and He let her know that she had something good to give to Him—no more than a cool drink of water, but something! Jesus was able to establish between them a relationship of understanding that paved the way for Him to give to her the Living Water. Different backgrounds, different races, different understandings of the way to live, and yet, He found where she was, and that's where He began.

EXPERIMENT—Stage Four

Objective: To look beyond the hooks, and tars, and unseen scars that keep us from understanding each other, and to find a starting place for sharing the Living Water.

We will see no one today who does not have some kind of problem. For just this short span of time we will pretend that we have none ourselves and will wonder what the other person's difficulty is. If it should be physical, we will offer a little of our strength; if we think it is anxiety, then we will give him a chance to unburden his heart to us; if we decide that he isn't aware of God's love, then, oh then, we will find a way to tell him.

CHAPTER 5

Too Big to Cry?

WHY IS IT that from the time children are able to understand, we begin to insist that they are "too big to cry"? They break their wagons, scratch their knees, cut their fingers, and, invariably, we try to stop their tears with words like these, "Sh-shu-shu-, don't cry, you're too big for that." Or, if we don't use this approach, there is another we unthinkingly insist upon, "Don't grieve over this trifle; it's nothing to cry about."

Our little boy could barely talk when he began to imitate the adult approach to an outward show of grief. If he bumped his head and the tears streamed, between each sob he would catch his breath long enough to say in his baby talk, "Nothing to ky about, nothing to ky about." Having made this profound observation, undoubtedly learned from us, he would then proceed to wail even louder. How did we know his hurt was nothing to cry about? How could we possibly measure the overwhelming grief of a small boy's heart?

Perhaps all parents must try to teach their children self-control in accepting pain and disappointment, but somehow we seem to have carried this attitude too far in our adult relationships with each other. "You're too big to cry," we tell ourselves, and go through occasions with a frigid mask upon our faces and feelings. "Nothing to cry about," we tell our hearts, and stifle emotion that God gave us as a sign that we care. You know what I mean; you have practiced ways, as I have, to keep from weeping where people can see. Pretend you have something in your eye; focus your thoughts on other subjects; plan your schedule for tomorrow; go over in your mind the bulbs and seeds you will add to your garden; think about anything, everything, that will keep you from showing other people that you are touched inside.

Now, self-control is one thing; frozen response is another. If you and I embark upon an experiment in human understanding, sheep-feeding, loving our neighbor, or whatever we want to call it, then we must consider this all-important aspect of grief— ours, and other people's. We must overcome this feeling that any show of emotion or admission of caring is immature.

Look at the first few verses in the third chapter of Ecclesiastes and find a basis for balance in Christian thinking. (Incidentally, these are more words that we read mostly for dying, not often enough for living.)

"To every thing there is a season, and a time to every purpose under the heaven: a time to be born, and a time to die; a time to plant, and a time to pluck up that which is planted; a time to kill, and a time to heal; a time to break down, and a time to build up; a time to weep, and a time to laugh; a time to mourn, and a time to dance . . ."

Christian balance! Ah, there's a hard assignment, yet the glorious thing about it is that Christ in us is the leveling factor! "A time to weep, and a time to laugh"—this is the small part of such balance that you and I will attempt to practice presently.

Somehow, we get along better with the laughing times, don't we? And this is true not only with our own joys but in being able to share the happy times of others. We are never too big to laugh, to show excited, happy appreciation and joy. These are mature, natural expressions that we can share while the going's good, while the heart is gay. A time to laugh, now this we understand, this we outwardly subscribe to.

But a time to weep! Oh, my dear, this is the hide-inside, shut-the-door, draw-the-shades, leave-alone, choke-back-the-tears time for most of us, be the grief ours or our fellow man's. I don't believe that Jesus meant for us to be this way. He wept, outwardly, openly, and sincerely, over the suffering of Mary and Martha when Lazarus died. As He looked out over the city of Jerusalem He grieved deeply, humanly, because of the indifference of the people He loved. He knew the time to weep. It should never be called "giving in to grief" as though it should be rejected and suppressed. Isn't it better to say "accepting grief" and letting God use it to His glory? Jesus wept. He actually cried where people could see, and His friends were strengthened in knowing that He shared their burdens.

Here is where we must change to help and be helped through Christian love. Don't ignore the hurt, ours or another's; don't pretend it isn't there; don't refuse to join hearts in open sorrow, for God can draw us close, so very close, through the mixing of our tears. We can be sure that laughter never travels alone, but looking very honestly, we discover that sorrow has the tendency to isolate its lodging.

Do you know the story of the two little girls who sat on the front steps weeping? When one was asked why she cried, she quickly answered, "Oh, I'm crying 'cause Polly's crying." She didn't need a reason beyond her friend's tears; she had only to know that Polly grieved. They bore the burden together, and surely it wasn't long before Polly looked past her own trouble and cared enough for her friend to seek to lift the spirits of such love. That's the way grief can shift the focus from ourselves to the strengthening of another who shows us that he cares.

Before our Experiment can be in any way termed successful, you and I will have to get over our childhood idea of being too big to cry and see that it really takes quite a grown-up, loving heart to face grief openly. To let God use our sorrows for good requires a "bigness" we will have to work toward.

What about human understanding with regard to the griefs of others? We don't always recognize the dreadful hurt or the brushed-away tear, do we? We have trained ourselves to see happy things, not those that will depress our spirits. This mental optimism is fine for feeding the happy little lambs that play in the sun upon a grassy hillside. But Jesus said to care also for the sheep that have strayed away, those that have been hurt, those that have fallen into the crevice between the jagged rocks along the way. He tells us to feed them. How can we possibly reach out to them if we do not go where they are, if we will not enter their prison in the dismal cave of sadness? So let's face it. Grieving sheep need nourishment in a very special way that demands an understanding of what sorrow is like.

In a large auditorium I sat behind a woman who had an ugly red scar reaching from her skull to beyond the low neckline of her dress. From the front she was a beautiful, serene, happy person with no problems or troubles; from the back she was as distorted and afflicted as physical grief could fashion her. A voice within me cried out, "Oh, you poor thing! How you must have suffered as you lay on your face the many weeks it took to heal your hurt. How intense your pain!" And then another voice, perhaps a little deeper in the part of me God's Spirit rules, insisted, "Yes, her physical grief demands your sympathy, but let not your understanding and compassion go only with your eyes. There are other forms of human suffering we must depend upon our hearts to see. Look around you tonight in this vast gathering of human personalities and know that, at one time or another, suffering and grief will be borne by each person here. Your challenge, as a Christian who has finally learned that nothing really matters except God and people, is to seek some way to share the burdens of grief, the visible kind and the kind you cannot see."

Consider it awhile. You'll soon decide that sorrow can be experienced in at least three ways.

There is physical suffering. Sometimes it can end, can be over and done with. Sometimes it is finished only when the body is discarded and the soul soars with God. It is intense, it is hard to bear, but it does have an advantage over the other kinds. As a rule it is admitted and confronted. Physical sorrow is usually easy to recognize. The woman's scar was like a banner waving my sympathy to attention.

There is mental suffering that makes no outward display of the grief within. We can understand this kind fairly well, even though we do not always detect it in others. We have felt the pain of worry; we have spent days in the company of the cancerous sore of anxiety. We have often struggled with the burden of doubt or mistrust weighting down our conscious and subconscious minds until sleeplessness and loss of appetite have taken their toll in sickness of the body. Oh, yes, we know what mental grief is like in ourselves, so it should not be too difficult to become aware that many people we meet are consumed with this kind of sorrow also. Jesus never tells us to cure the diseases of our brothers; He merely asks us to walk along beside them, to help them bear their loads, to let them know we are there. As remarkable as it may seem, oftentimes someone to listen is the cure for this kind of burden.

And then there is spiritual suffering, which is different from the others because it's deeper. It involves a separation, an emptiness that must wait to be filled. No miraculous cure, no sudden understanding, no pat answer, will ever lessen the pain of a grieving spirit. It must wait, not for the broken heart to be healed but for God's grace, for the therapy of His days and nights and weeks, and months, and even years, to open up new chambers of the soul.

A woman sat in our living room and quite calmly stated a fact that she had learned from experience: "Sometimes, sometimes, it is so much easier to die than to live." Grief had emptied her, but she was waiting expectantly, even patiently, for God to refill new areas of her being and lead her into new ways of glorifying Him as she accepted this sorrow.

The loss of a loved one can make this scar. The betrayal and denial of a trusted friend can cause this lonely emptiness of separation. Perhaps we haven't met this kind of sorrow, but surely there is one way to grasp a glimpse of what this brand of suffering is like. Let your mind dwell on the time when Jesus watched Judas leave the upper room to sell His love. How do you suppose our Lord stood the emptiness, the loss, and the heartbreak of the separation of that moment? Or how does He feel as we, who bear His name, cling stubbornly to a known sin that blocks us off from complete commitment to Him? The bitterness of this grief cannot be understood until we taste a portion of it ourselves, but it can be recognized in others by a child of God who strives to be aware.

So, as difficult as it is for both of us, you and I must respond to sorrow, must be willing to let God use our sadnesses to some good and for other people. We must strengthen our caring to the point that we will never run from the griefs of others, but will walk willingly and lovingly along the way with them. To become aware of the deepest feelings of another person fulfills the purpose of our being. It completes the triangle God has planned: Himself loving me, me loving you, we together loving Him.

A man and his wife boarded a crowded train. Having experienced a deep and tragic grief, they seemed to cling to each other for strength with which to go on. They looked bewildered as they stood at the end of the car searching frantically for two seats together. Finding none, the man helped his wife to the nearest vacancy and took his place in another part of the car. As the woman settled back, resigned to enduring the long ride alone, she felt a hand on her arm. "I would like to exchange places with your husband, so that the two of you may be together," came the voice from the adjoining seat. A stranger had somehow sensed the pain and wanted to help bear the burden of a person she would never see again. A woman of another race was aware that grief can be shared even by those whose lives touch only for a moment. "Let me help in the only way I can," she was trying to say, "for I feel your weight of sorrow. I care about you." With a grateful heart the wife accepted the gift of friendship. The other woman, a Negro, whose love knew no barrier, found comfort in the fact that all during the long journey, and even as they left the train, the wife held tightly to her husband's hand.

Share laughter, share joys, share wonderful, happy experiences that will bind you close to other people. But let not your sharing end here. You are never too big to cry when your tears are honest, compassionate, humble expressions of your caring.

God has a way of lifting my heart,
When sorrow and despair
Have pushed it down into the mire
And left it grieving there.

God has a way of healing my heart,
Of causing it to mend.
He does it not with might or force,
God does it with a friend.

EXPERIMENT—Stage Five

OBJECTIVE: To face grief openly as a part of being a person who cares, and to let others know that their grief is shared by us.

Today, if sadness presents itself in understandable or in elusive, puzzling forms, let us try to meet it; try to express companionship that causes a sorrowful heart to realize that we care. But, just to be sure that we practice this new attitude toward our brother's burden, let us think back to a time when we failed to reach out to a grieving heart. This will not be hard to do. You and I daily miss opportunities to express concern. We will pick out only one of these people with whom we failed to walk the path of sadness. Now let us find a way to offer loving sympathy. Maybe it will require a visit, a telephone call, a sincere letter expressing not how we think we ought to feel but how we truly join our hearts and prayers with theirs in dealing with the hurt. We will surely be faced with the same obstacle that caused us to miss the earlier opportunity, but this time we will overcome it. Maybe it will take a pie from our kitchen, roses from our garden, a book from our shelf, to make a bridge over which we cross the barriers in our way. But, whatever it takes, you and I must find it to complete the triangle of God's love. And some day, we might understand that unhappiness we endure prepares us to reach out with comfort to others who must cry.

CHAPTER 6

God's Plan for a Man

I MUST BE HONEST with you. This is the chapter that I had to begin all over again at least three times. Do you suppose it's because this step of the Experiment is the most difficult one for me?

Consider two facts that at first thought seem in no way related at all. One: in this world there is nothing that belongs solely or completely to one individual. Two: in this world there is nothing whose beginning or end we can see in its entirety.

Much of our unhappiness stems from continued belief in the opposite of these two truths. We don't ever like to admit it, but in our secret hearts we set ourselves up in place of God and judge how life ought to be, how it should turn out. Then we cannot understand why things don't go according to our plan. We decide what things and people and events belong to us, saying, "This is mine; no one else has any right to this, my experience, my possessions, my home, my baby, my life." Wouldn't we be saved great heartache and disappointment if we could see relationships in the proper perspective? Wouldn't we live much more harmoniously with others if we could realize that our ownership in anything is interwoven with other people, and if we could just let God be in charge of how things turn out?

Once we understand that all God wants is our loving Him enough to include other people, it is very simple to see how He made His world to be shared. He didn't make the sun for you and the moon for me; He made them, both of them, for both of us! Begin here and move on to more complicated possessions.

Your money? Is it ever only yours, whether it be stashed away in the bank or paid out for toothpaste or taxes or tango lessons? Aren't other people involved? The bank uses it until you spend it; the very act of buying something brings in everybody else. In whatever form it is, however you save it or scatter it abroad, your money is dealt with by many other individuals.

Your graduation? Look into the eyes of your father who did without to pay the bills, your mother who surrounded each step of the way with concern and prayer, your teachers who gave you a part of themselves to make your diploma possible. It's their graduation too.

Your operation? Is it yours or the surgeon's who spent twenty-six years preparing to use the knife? Or does it belong to the nurse who accepted long hours of drudgery to become skillful and sure? Your wedding, your friends, your family, your troubles, all are other people's too. Experiences, joys, sorrows, even they can never be yours alone. "What right has he to interfere? Why can't she mind her own business? What's it to you?" we say, never stopping long enough to analyze the situation, never realizing that God entwines our lives in ways that can never be untangled. She cannot mind her own business for it is like the sun and the moon: her business belongs directly or indirectly to us. To understand each other, to mean more to each other, to reach out to each other, we must see that nothing belongs completely to us alone, that everything is a part of God's creation planned by Him for us.

Oh, dear, we decide, that puts us in a pretty responsible place, doesn't it? That really mixes our lives up with those all around us! It does, and for this reason every minute of every day can be a glorious challenge. It can, if we remember that to complete the triangle there must be a third side—other people.

There was a silly saying we enjoyed many years ago. I don't remember where it began, but I do remember that it never could be finished. It was an imaginary conversation between two people that went something like this:

"You remind me of a man."

"What man?"

"The man with the power."

"What power?"

"The power of Houdu."

"Houdu?"

"You do."

"Do what?"

"Remind me of a man."

"What man?"

"The man with the power." And on and on and on as long as we could stand it. The thing that impressed us was that this could go on forever, that it was a tricky dialogue in which each statement prompted a question which in turn was answered by another statement that prompted another question, a continuing process to which there was no end. How much better off we

would be if we could realize that God's world is planned with
this no-ending factor as a basic truth!

One of our greatest difficulties in human relations is that we
set ourselves up as being capable of deciding how things must
turn out. We want to see results, we desire to be *in* on the
outcome, we demand that life work out according to our pre-
conceived idea. We cannot bear not being able to see the end
as we plan it. We dare to make decisions as though we were
God, saying quite frankly to Him, "You know best, but look
here, this is what I hope you'll do."

I have a friend whose wife was expecting a baby. The father
prayed earnestly for God's blessing and care for the mother
and the child. His prayer, so typically human, was thus: "O
God, in Your divine wisdom You can see what's best for us.
Whether You give us a son or a daughter is for You to decide.
I pray that the baby will be healthy and Mary will get along
fine. Just bring our baby here safely is all I ask. It's up to You,
Lord, whether it is a boy or a girl. Thy will be done. But, O
Lord, You know my preference."

God wants people. He wants them for a reason, a purpose,
His reason, His purpose. And yet we are continually wanting
things to turn out or end up our way. Remember how all fairy
stories end "and they all lived happily ever after"? As children
we considered this the best part. Something in us delights in
seeing the finish and pronouncing it good or bad. But this is
not our part; it is God's. Much of our trouble where other people
are concerned stems from putting our judgment above God's
and concluding that we know how to end things happily ever
after.

When you get right down to the truth of the matter we never
actually see the beginning or the end of anything, do we? A
newborn baby inherits characteristics from his great-great-grand-
father. A man dies, and even if there were no life beyond, the
man lives on in his deeds, his words, his children, and ways we

cannot determine with our finite minds. Burn wood and you still have ashes; scatter the ashes and they remain somewhere. God's world is so perfectly interwoven, one aspect with another, that even scientific equipment cannot determine the actual beginning or the ultimate end of anything. Yet we still deceive ourselves by saying that this didn't turn out right, or that his life was a success, or that she wasted her opportunities.

Do you admit that what I am saying about us is true? We see only little, outward, here-and-now portions of people. We experience only tiny sections of God's universe and time, yet we are foolish enough to think that we know how things ought to be. Let's acknowledge this to be a prime factor in our failure to understand and love other people. And all mixed in with this misconception is the other fallacy that we can separate what belongs to us from the possessions of our fellow man.

How many times in the life of Peter would we have pointed out to Jesus that He had picked the wrong man? If it had been possible, how quickly and confidently we would have tactfully said to Jesus, "Oh, do be careful, Lord. Peter isn't all that You think he is. Surely You don't plan to build Your church on him or give him the keys to the kingdom of heaven! He has You completely fooled, duped. Watch out for him! In spite of his confession, Peter is the very one who will deny You, not once but three times. He is not strong like a rock, not steady enough to be the beginning of a church, especially my church. Why, I want my church to be the best, the most successful, the wealthiest, with the most influential people as members. Don't pick Peter, Lord, to start my church. He is just a common fisherman who acts without thinking, whose response is quick but whose leadership is untrained." Now had we lived in those days, wouldn't we have thought these things even though we found not the courage to say them? You see, we couldn't know the end; we observe only a brief portion of eternity's span of time and we make our judgment as final as if we were God.

Nothing has completely turned out yet, for nothing has ended so far as God's plan is concerned. And who are we to know, to see, to love, enough to say, "Not Peter; he represents failure in its lowest form"? This failure turned to triumph of a mighty kind. Read the book of Acts and you'll learn part of what happened to Peter. Oh, yes, he came to "no good end," for tradition says he was crucified too, you know. But Peter has not finished yet, not yet. Whenever the church is the living Body of our crucified Lord, Peter's faith and life continue to strengthen your church and mine. And we would have written him off as being a poor choice.

Read the prayer of Jesus as He faces the Cross (John 17). Can you feel the confidence and trust that He has in those eleven men? He offers them to God, saying, "I have guarded them, and none of them is lost . . ." (John 17:12). To us they may seem to be weak, jealous, ineffectual men who will flee at the first signs of danger. To Jesus, they are the hope of the world.

Therefore, to make our love for God really count, to offer it to Him in a usable form where other people are concerned, to allow Him to use us as a positive force in His creation, we must voluntarily get off the pedestal of self-esteem. We must get down to a place from which we can look upward to see Jesus, and outward to understand, through love, His other children.

EXPERIMENT—Stage Six

Objective: To look at all events and things as interlocking pieces of God's world, which we do not control but enjoy.

As we meet people today let us remind ourselves: "They are a part of a wonderful creation. Their lives and mine are all bound together in ways I cannot name. God is using them for His purpose in methods I cannot see. My part is not to judge, nor to predict the ultimate outcome, but to love simply, sincerely, steadily, knowing that God's hand will hold, now and in the ages to come." Then, perhaps as we walk along, or ride along, or work along we can play a mental game with words like these:

God has a plan.
What plan?
His plan for man.
What man?
A man with a brother.
What brother?
A brother of another.
Another what?
Another man in the plan.
What plan?
God's plan for man.
What man?
A man with a brother . . . and on, and on, and on.

CHAPTER 7

Christian Communication

"Beasts and birds of every kind, creatures that crawl on the ground or swim in the sea, can be subdued and have been subdued by mankind; but no man can subdue the tongue. It is an intractable evil, charged with deadly venom. We use it to sing the praises of our Lord and Father, and we use it to invoke curses upon our fellow-men who are made in God's likeness. Out of the same mouth come praises and curses. My brothers, this should not be so" (James 3: 7-10).

MY BROTHERS and my sisters in Christ, this cannot be so if you and I are serious about our Experiment in understanding. Praise God and curse our fellow man! We are beginning to see that this combination of feelings is impossible, aren't we? We simply cannot worship God on our terms. It must be according to His stipulations, His rules. Jesus stated these very clearly, saying, "If you love me, what I care about you must also care about—other people."

No doubt you are thinking, "You've said that before." Sometimes it takes many rephrasings of the same idea to get it into our all-time consciousness. This is not a fact to be learned or a concept to be taken from the mind and used when necessary. This is a truth to be lived by every one of us who answers His searching question with: "Yes, Lord, Thou knowest that I love Thee."

The writer of James certainly puts his finger on a vulnerable spot in our personal relations. Undoubtedly the tongue is a treacherous, unruly factor in the discipline of a heart pledged to God. Yet we cannot take the attitude that words are wicked witches to be chained. We cannot guard every relationship with a sign posted in the front yards of our minds saying, "Beware of the tongue!" No, we must find some way to glory in Christian communication, be it clothed in the audible, or the readable, or the feelable language of love.

Perhaps we should begin by thinking through the unlimited power of communication. It is the food on which all human relations depend. Look at our wide, wide world that suddenly becomes a quarrelsome family, living in what seems to be overcrowded quarters. Did communications contribute? Consider the whole process of education. Is communication important? See a man and a woman begin a home together. Will communication have a part in their success or failure? It overwhelms us to realize how vital this interchange of ideas can be, how necessary it is that hopes, fears, moods, be understood wherever there are people. We cannot overestimate the importance of the outward expression of the inward man as it becomes a prime factor in friendship or enmity, in individuals or in nations.

So we are agreed that this business of revealing outwardly what we actually feel inwardly is an all-important aspect in living together.

Three times I had called our little boy to supper. When he finally pulled himself away from his play and faced the guilt of tardiness, he ran into the kitchen saying, "How are you looking, Mother? Let me see how you are looking." Our faces can show in one instant what it takes many words to say. These expressions can be powerful in positive ways, in happy, friendly, understanding ways. The face does not have to be beautiful in terms of magazine-cover standards to give a lovely outward message of an inward caring grace.

How we are looking makes a difference to start with in our communication system. Oftentimes the warmest feelings come from a smile, a handshake, a gesture that says in ways words cannot, "You and I are kin. We are members of God's family. You have a definite worth, and I love you and respect you for it."

Awareness of the other person! This seems to be the basic quality that will temper the response, guide the tongue, strengthen the relationship. My eyes and yours, my smile and yours, can express this awareness without a single uttered sound.

Once we get this true concern for others, then the words we speak or write, or those that we do not speak or write, will fall into His pattern of caring. Here again Christian balance is our goal. "A time to keep silence, and a time to speak . . ." (Ecclesiastes 3:7) will be understood by an individual to whom others make a difference. To weigh every word with great thought and deliberation would often cause us to miss the opportunity, to let the chance slip by. This world of ours rushes frantically on, unmindful that we might decide to express ourselves, doesn't it? But, with true concern for every individual as the motivation for our speaking, we can rely on God's Holy Spirit to frame our utterances in a way that is acceptable and heartwarming to others.

Let us recognize that the tongue is powerful and pray to use it wisely. Recognizing its full potential, we will suddenly become mindful of the strength of a small piece of equipment in your house and mine.

As far back as 1796 the Greeks had a word for "sound from afar" which was the beginning of our telephone. It's hard to imagine what life would be like without this amazing contraption which in a few short years has become a definite necessity. I cannot believe that Alexander Graham Bell had any idea of the magnitude or importance of his invention. If you can't remember the first hand-grinding wall models, you probably cannot appreciate the present eight decorator colors, the executive extensions, the over-the-shoulder no-hands type, the fancy French one-piece kind, or the riding-along automobile miracles. These might not impress you, but can you learn that there are over one hundred million telephones in the world and not agree that they do have a big part in human relations?

In the days of the silent movies, there was a peculiar art in transmitting ideas by being seen and not heard. Today, there is just as great an art in being understood when you are heard and not seen. Some businessmen make and lose huge fortunes over the telephone. Some phones save lives, others directly or indirectly destroy them. Some people use phones to build, others use them to tear down. How to control a telephone? Why, it is just as necessary to know this as how to balance your daily diet.

Now look at your small piece of equipment with greater respect, saying, "You are a powerful tool of mine, made of strange materials like palladium, ferrite, quartz crystals, and copper. You reach out through networks of wires, lines, cables, relays, exchanges, that I can never understand. But in spite of all this, I am your master. I can use you as I please. I can make you a beast or a blessing, a curse or a champion, a delight or a demon. Which shall I choose to turn you into today?"

That makes you pretty powerful, doesn't it? That makes you the fairy godmother or the dreadful dragon. That gives you an unbelievable influence to bring glory to God or shame to His children.

Consider this conversation: "Hello. As I passed your house and saw your beautiful flowers, I felt God very near"; or this one, "I am counting my blessings today, and I'm so thankful for your friendship"; or, "Someone paid you a wonderful compliment and I wanted you to know it"; or, "I rejoiced with you today as you joined our church." Does that kind of use of the telephone mean anything to the person who is just beginning to understand what love of God does to a human heart? It is sure to draw him closer. This is your power, yours and God's.

There is another means of communication open to us that many never use. We just don't realize the value of written-down words. We don't understand the treasure that letters become to some people, who guard them as carefully as pearls of great price, as living companions in the lonely times.

I had a friend who lived in a nursing home the last few years of her life. Every time I visited her, she went through the same procedure.

"Hand me the box," she would say, and I would know exactly what she meant. On a table by her bed, a discolored old candy box held all of the valuables she possessed. Her frail bony hands would almost snatch the box from mine, and I would wait while she fumbled with the top. Then, one by one, she would take out her letters and hand them to me to read.

"From Mary, from Joe, from Cousin Hattie," she would declare, as though I had never read those fading lines before. Her weak body required very little nourishment, but her hungry heart was as a starving spirit clutching at every crumb of food. When she would come to the hurried letters and cards I had sent, she would smile with affection, and I would be so ashamed. The last hours she spent were brightened by a faded, soiled candy box with a few old postmarked envelopes containing the treasures of her life.

Written-down words can be feasted upon, over and over

again. Written-down words can be medicine, taken whenever the patient is in need. Written-down words can lift a lonely, discouraged soul closer to a knowledge of God.

So, there we have it, a realization that our communication systems must function properly if we are to fulfill our purposes, if we are to reach out in love.

EXPERIMENT—Stage Seven

Objective: To use more effectively the power of personal communication.

We will go to our telephones and make three calls today— after we pray. One of these will join us to a friend who has recently recovered from a serious illness and needs a tonic for the spirit. One of these will be to an acquaintance who has lost a loved one and needs to cure the loneliness left hanging in his heart. The third will be to a person we dislike. We will be determined to use this means to express love.

We will write a letter today to someone who needs a treasure to keep by her bed or to place carefully in her Bible. We will pretend that we are with her and that she says to us, "Hand me the box." We will make our letters the kind that are worth reading and rereading as the ink begins to fade. If we should have trouble finding thoughts worthy of such treatment, on our next trip to the stationery store we will seek a special little assortment of cards and notepaper with tender messages of hope and affection. We will use these for a while, finding daily opportunity to send our love to someone out of touch. We will only start the cure for loneliness; God will surely finish it.

the "Specials" in your Life

 USTER IS QUITE a character! He is a pathetic, delight-ful, amazing creature all in one. Paralytic polio left the little boy barely able to move about in braces reaching to his waist. An immature, unstable mother left him to be shifted around from one foster home to the next. All of it together had made him a wise old character at the age of eight. My association with him through the Crippled Children's Clinic was painful and joyous at the same time.

During our many trips to the doctor, Buster and I discussed

quite a few subjects. Usually I was the one who learned something.

"Are you saved?" he asked me one day after blowing the horn of my automobile until even he was ready to stop.

"Yes, Buster," I said. "I'm saved because I believe in Jesus Christ who died for me. Are you saved?"

"Yup, I am, but my Mama ain't. I pray every night that my Mama will repent and git baptized. Brother George, he says that hit's the only thing I can do. Hit's mighty important that she don't have to go to hell."

"Who is Brother George?" I asked, hoping to avoid a heated discussion of you-know-where.

"Brother George is my preacher, and Brother George says that my Mama is shore going to hell if she don't . . . !"

"Is Brother George a good preacher?" I interrupted hastily.

"Sure, he's a good preacher," declared Buster. "He thows the gospel at us, and I mean he thows it hard. I can't decide whether I'm gonna be a preacher when I git big, or if I'll jist lead the singing. Brother George, he does both. Can I blow the horn again?"

And once I had been informed as to the great abilities of Brother George, there was rarely a visit with Buster that he did not discuss the last sermon, or the recent athletic feat, or the latest joke from his trusted friend and pastor. In all of that little boy's uncertain world, one person never failed him; in one relationship he was never disappointed. Why? Do you think it is because Brother George is perfect? No, he's just an average country preacher doing the best he can. But the reason he is ten feet tall in Buster's mind is that Buster looks at him with eyes of love and finds the answer to his need. So the minister is a "special" person to Buster, one who belongs to him.

In a sense, all ministers are our special people, as are doctors, and teachers, and, sometimes, a very unusual friend. They are put in an area of our hearts reserved just for them. They are our personal property to be dealt with in whatever way we choose.

Before you protest that this isn't true, think about how much these people mean to you; about the things you ask of them that no one else can offer; about the relationship you have with them requiring their continuous giving to you. Of course you pay them for professional service, but is the financial transaction between you the basis on which their help is rendered? You know it isn't. We cannot buy a minister or a doctor or a teacher; yet without the slightest qualm we treat them as if they were registered in our name. We seem to forget that they are people too; we overlook their right to have a different opinion, or to be mistaken, or to get very, very tired.

It's important that we consider this relationship, because, quite often, in making these people more than human we demand too much and turn away critical or disgruntled. Since they don't prove to be supermen, we judge that they have failed. And then we tread on dangerous ground. By critical disapproval we lessen the effectiveness of their influence on others who need them too. The body, the mind, the spirit, add up to the complete man. The doctor, the teacher, the minister, are caught up in human relations in ways that make them unique to every one of us.

If we become successful in reaching out with compassion, the Experiment must include the "specials" in our lives. Their full-time business and life work is people. We join in partnership with them, attempting to understand and care. So let us, like Buster, look at them with eyes of love.

Look at the minister. Have we ever been guilty of painting a perfect picture in our minds and saying, "Now this is what a minister should be like. Where, oh where, can I find such a man?" Suppose we examine our little boy, or our little brother. A minister is no more than a grown-up one of these.

These little boys bit their nails, wanted the biggest piece of pie, cried when their pride was hurt, fought for the seat beside the car window, hated to admit that they had failed to shut the barn door, fairly swelled with pride when they accomplished a hard task, showed off when company came, made mistakes in grammar, didn't know exactly how to say they were sorry. All of these things our little boys or brothers were. And now that they are men, are they any less human? Are they any less individuals with fears and fallacies, with peculiarities and problems, with anxieties and ambitions? We don't expect them to change all of these aspects of their personalities, do we?

Then, why do we expect a minister (who is somebody's little boy or big brother grown up) to be a completely different species from other human beings? Going to a seminary is a pretty rugged deal, but not quite that rugged! Why, if you and I had our way, we would melt down regular normal boys, pour them into a mold, and, when cool, take out a minister for each congregation. And what do we expect the cookie-press, or the cutting machine, or the preacher-mold to produce?

We want a mature, settled, experienced pastor, who appears and acts, and is able to work, like a young college athlete. We want him to look like a man of distinction but never to seem to be concerned with the superficiality of style. We want him to clothe his wife and children in keeping with the tastes of the congregation, but we pay him about half what we spend on ourselves. We want him to be an intellectual giant, but we never give him an uninterrupted time for study.

We expect him to rejoice over every happiness that we find, every A or B+ that Johnny gets, and we want him to show genuine grief over the passing of our Great-aunt Susie whom he has never met.

We want our minister to be right there on the spot if we feel fear, or loneliness, or sometimes just plain boredom, but we hope he has sense enough not to drop in when something that's none of his business goes on in our home.

We expect him to give advice whenever we ask it, and if things don't turn out right, well, then it's his fault. If matters proceed successfully, then it was our idea all along. He just happened to agree.

We demand that he understand what it is to be an alcoholic, how it feels to have a nervous breakdown, what it's like to be divorced, even though none of these things could possibly be permitted to a minister. Still, he must understand.

We ask him to organize, to promote, to build. Then we tell him to stick to the preaching and leave the money to the deacons. We require him to be available for consultation at all hours, and we complain that he did not drop by when we had our tooth pulled.

We ask him to preach meaningful sermons, those that we can grow by, but woe, woe, is he if he mentions brotherhood, or business ethics, or corrupt government, or Sabbath observance, or social drinking, in or out of the pulpit. We ask him to teach the Bible to us, and we leave it entirely in his hands, never thinking of digging in a little for ourselves. We expect him to be letter-perfect theologically, Biblically, grammatically, and in addition to all that, to finish his sermon at exactly twelve o'clock, if not a little before!

Now I ask you, is that fair? Is that possible? Is that human understanding? It is not. It definitely is not.

Remember this about your minister. He is a little boy or a big brother grown up—one who has admitted he is a sinner, just as we are; one who continuously needs God, just as we do; one who has said and meant with all his heart, "Lord, take me, and use me as Thou wilt." And maybe *we* haven't truly done that. He has thought it out and concluded that next to God, other people are all that matter. He has staked his life on that! And then we dare to be critical and indifferent and sometimes, oh, sometimes, openly hostile.

Look at your minister with eyes of love and you'll be surprised at what you see. His gentleness that makes little children know he is their friend, his spiritual strength that invites the confidence of each member of his flock, his undaunted courage that keeps him trying day after day of seeming to get nowhere, his willingness to listen to your troubles when he has so many of his own— these are the qualities that make your minister become your elder brother, if you'll accept him as a person "sent from God" who is not the Light, but who comes to bear witness of that Light in every way he can.

What would happen if your minister knew that he could always count on your willingness to learn, to grow, to pray, to give, and to love? What would happen? Something wonderful! Why, your Brother George would "thow the gospel at you," not just in church but in your whole wonderful new relationship— and I mean he'd "thow" it hard! You and he and God together would tackle any problem, even those as big as Buster's.

Look at the doctor. We might have several in these days of specialization, but surely there is one whom we consider our very special property. We tell him every ache and pain. We find his listening ear and attentive mind sympathetic to all kinds of trouble. We feel that he must be waiting right by the telephone, in the office, or at the dinner table, whenever we might decide to call. Unconsciously, we think of him as a man who has no objective until we turn to him saying, "This is my problem, solve it." He is "ours" in very much the same sense as the minister, the first one we seek out when things go wrong. And that is as it should be, provided we give him credit for being a person too.

Years ago, struggling with our first baby's colic, we overdid our concern as most parents do. The young doctor who answered our calls for help was a third parent to our wakeful infant. He instructed us in the fine points of successful ways to burp a baby; he juggled the Karo syrup content in the tedious daily formula; he even taught us how to administer castor oil, an accomplishment completely lost in the modern approach to medicine. How he stood our continual demands I do not know. Something that his wife said gave me sudden insight into the fact that he was a parent of his child, too. Laughingly, she confided to me, "Last night, when you called asking what to do about your baby's constant crying, I was amused at John. He told you to put the baby to bed and let her scream. Then he hung up the phone and continued walking the floor with our baby until she went to sleep."

Doctors are people, our people, with such compassion, and ability, and tired, tired bodies. Yet, you and I who count on them to make things better for us, often make things worse for them.

You might not believe what actually happened to one of our doctor friends. You might not admit that people can be so terribly unfair, unless you think back to times when you've been just as selfish in a little different way.

Early one night "Doc" got a call from a patient who lived several miles out in the country. "Come at once," the husband said; "my wife has been bitten by a poisonous snake." The man owed for many previous visits, but "Doc" refused to let a snake bite go unattended and good-naturedly drove the distance to their home. The woman's ankle was without swelling or redness, having two tiny marks that looked suspiciously selfmade. "Doc" asked questions, gave his verdict that nothing was wrong, and packed his bag, ready to start the long trip home. The husband put on his coat. "Would you give me a ride back to town?" he asked. Then he added, "I need to go, and it's cheaper having you come than calling a taxi."

Perhaps we've never done just this kind of thing. Perhaps we have limited our mistreatment to more subtle time-consuming, demanding ways that overlook the doctor's obligations to so many other people, to his own family, and to himself.

Teachers? They are like the others in their dedication and in their right to be considered human beings too. Undoubtedly lack of voiced, visible, and sincere appreciation is about the greatest way in which we fail them, even a larger injustice than financial underpayment.

In my early days of bridal cooking, I would often ask my husband, "Didn't you like the dinner? You haven't said a word of praise." I would always get the classic answer jokingly, "If I don't say anything, you'll know it's all right. I'll let you know when anything isn't good."

That's how we treat teachers, and not jokingly. It is when Johnny is not doing well or we are not satisfied with his treatment that we bother to contact the teacher. Only when we are asked to teach a Sunday school class do we pay tribute to the week after week dedication that teaching takes by saying lamely, "Oh, no, I'm not good enough."

Teachers are ever so important. There are a thousand reasons why; we know them without making a list. Encouragement, cooperation, stimulation, respect, honest-to-goodness friendliness, can turn a poor teacher into a good teacher, and a good one into an invaluable influence in the lives of so many people, people we have begun to care about.

EXPERIMENT—Stage Eight

Objective: To see our "special people" in a new light, realizing their contributions to a community of needy and searching souls.

Find a way to reach out to your minister in love. Find a way to tell him that you are thankful for his willingness to serve God and man. Find a way to make him the promise that daily you will ask God to guide him in all he does. Offer your support to him in a new sense, saying, "Here is my intellect which reaches to learn. Here is my strength which is willing to sustain. And here, O my minister, is my love that can be counted on to forgive faults and to nourish abilities, as you and I undertake this marvelous venture together."

Get word to your doctor by phone, or by notepaper, or by chocolate cream pie, that whenever he can use your help in the problems of other patients (be it transportation, babysitting, or just a listening ear) you will count it a privilege to help in any way you can. Be certain he understands that you are thankful for his care.

Pick out one teacher and let her know that you appreciate the great contributions that teachers make to a community. How to do it? A person who loves God with all his heart can surely find a way.

Attempt these things, and I will too. Perhaps new awareness will be the outcome.

the Church without a Wall

NCE UPON A TIME the people built a beautiful church. Its steeple could be seen for miles around, and its chimes rang out in glorious notes of praise to God. Dignified splendor clothed its sanctuary; its many classrooms were complete in every detail. Outside the church were gardens with flowers and green grass, play yards for the children, and underneath the trees the parents could relax with congenial friends. It was a lovely church, once you went inside its walls. Oh, yes, there were walls, high brick ones, taller than a man or boy could climb. It was only through one gate that people could enter the domain of the church. The gate was ajar most of the time, but not always could a person find that particular opening. Quite often those who wished to enter would go away disappointed, for the wall was all that they could see. On Sunday mornings the members gathered, the choirs sang, the minister preached, and the people outside the walls did not know what a church was all about. *The people inside never knew either.*

You and I have walked a way of understanding together. We have thought of God and His love for us. We have attempted new experiences of response to His caring. But now we come to the gathering together of all He offers and all He asks. We must look at His divine institution, the church, prepared for us by Him. We cannot end our Experiment without a deeper realization that the church is concerned with people. It is a uniting of all who love Him in a relationship, unique and precious.

The church is not a building, not a program, not an organization for service. It regards not the limitations of man-made time schedules, or places-of-meeting, or ritualistic regulations. The church is the Body of Christ broken for all men who believe. It is the Blood of Christ shed for every person who accepts. It is the Love of Christ dependent upon no bricks or gates, or steeples in the sky. The church is Christ, requiring only the hearts of men in which to dwell.

One summer day we invited a Czechoslovakian family who attended our church to go on a picnic. They spoke very little English and had no idea what a picnic was, but Mama, Papa, and the two little boys climbed happily into our car. Just a few miles out of town, as we rode along a country road, one of the boys tugged at my sleeve. "Lady," he exclaimed, "this picnic, good." "No," I hurriedly answered, "this not picnic yet. Picnic, later." He looked puzzled but turned to enjoy the interesting sights we passed.

When we arrived at the state park, rented a rowboat, and

paddled out upon the lake, the other little boy turned to me with delight, saying, "Thank you, Lady, I like picnic." "No," I declared again, "picnic comes later." The boys looked questioningly at each other, said many words I couldn't understand, and then began to wave excitedly to all the other boats on the lake.

The pony rides were next. As I stood at the fence rail and watched the children ride around and around the pony circle, there was no doubt what they gleefully called over their shoulders to me as they passed. "Oh, Lady, Lady, picnic very okay, okay." And "Lady" muttered to herself, "No picnic yet, picnic later."

It was not until we sat around the table and enjoyed the fellowship of sharing food together that I could make my friends understand. "Listen to me," I said slowly as I looked from one to the other. "This, this is picnic." A smile came over Mama's face and she said, "Picnic, good." Papa said, "Picnic, I like." And the two little boys said almost together, "Oh, nice picnic, we come again."

Could it be that we often get the activities, the by-products, the methods of the church mixed up with its true meaning? Sometimes we see its program apart from the original purpose and say, "I must do this particular job, must attend this meeting, must establish some pattern of action, for this, this is the church." But it is not!

Perhaps as we teach little children in Sunday school we encourage ourselves along by saying, "This is the church." But it is not!

Even as we take our places at the eleven o'clock service and nod to our neighbors in the pew, we are mistaken in thinking, "This, this is my church." It is not!

These activities engaged in by us are not the church but are the results of the true meaning and purpose of it all. The church, strangely enough, can be likened to a picnic table, with you and me enjoying the shared fellowship of the redemptive love of Jesus Christ, our Lord. It is the breaking of the Bread of Life together, the uniting in a great thankfulness for Him together. Strangely enough, the church is not one man and God. It is made up of many members of the same Body, members who love Him so much that they must express this love toward others.

Now once you and I see this living, eternal membership in its true light we admit to ourselves that there is no way at all to experience love for God that does not react upon or reach out to other people. Then, oh, then, worshiping together in our church services, seeking God's blessing together, engaging in activities, accepting responsibilities, establishing programs and buildings, these become joyous expressions of our relationship to God. They become necessary nourishment to our growing love for other people. They are not the church but are the means by which we have a part in the accomplishment of its mission. They are the way we love and serve and tell.

Three people met to seek God's will,
They sought to do it well.
They planned for each to try one thing,
One love, one serve, one tell.

They went forth and with great zeal
One loved, one served, one told.
Then they met to check results,
To see God's plan unfold.

The one who loved, reporting first,
Confessed with great dismay,
"I couldn't keep from serving too.
Love knows no other way."

The one who served then bared his heart,
"I must admit it's true.
I couldn't serve until I loved.
So I did both things too."

The third, whose aim was to proclaim,
With wisdom did agree,
"You cannot separate each one,
For God combined all three.

"I tried to tell, but no one heard
Until God's love shone through.
And both of you proclaimed with deeds.
All three, we each must do."

The power of the church is there, but you and I must get a new conception of what the church is all about before we become conductors of the power. A lonely apartment, a white hushed hospital room, a screeching, noisy factory—all of these places become the church when people share Christ.

So let us knock down the walls around the building; let us take the church where people are, and bring them into our worshiping, serving fellowship. Let the steeple rise above, let the chimes ring out, let the people gather on a Sunday morning in a church without a wall.

EXPERIMENT—Stage Nine

Objective: To change our misconception that the church is an organization, a building, a program; to gain the knowledge that the Body of Jesus Christ is a living, sharing membership in the hearts of men.

We will select a person who seems completely unconscious of the church. Discarding all ideas we have about attendance, giving, and service being the objective, we will seek this person in love. Knowing full well that Jesus never made rules by which we can judge worthiness of membership, we will become conscious of our own undeserving natures and admit that for all men He died. As we seek this person outside the church we will not demand that he attend a definite meeting, or offer certain gifts. Later on, when he believes that we care about him, he will want to know the reason. Then will be our opportunity to make him understand that Jesus Christ is the reason, that He does make a difference. Surely God will lead this child of His to join with us in loving, and serving, and telling through the program of the church.

the Unrecognized Christ

*J*UST ONE MORE MATTER to settle, just one more step to take. Loving our neighbor as ourselves is the answer if we love God. If we love God . . .

This fellowship, this sharing of His Body, this communion in love—just how important is it to us? Well, it has to be one of two ways. Either it is the whole objective of our lives, or it isn't. Either this Jesus whom we have access to is our Savior, or He isn't. Either we profess Him wholeheartedly, or we betray His love. There can be no halfway, lukewarm in-between so far as our desire is concerned. Either we are full-time followers, who make our daily living Christian, or we merely take Him up on weekends as a hobby. The test is in the purpose, the choice that is made, rather than in the results as the world sees them.

By now we have reached the final stage and the decision is ours. If God is not our choice, then discount the previous procedures as meaningless games to be played in dull hours. If God is our desire, if we must respond to His love, then awareness of the greatest opportunities is our goal. Let us remember words that Jesus spoke and see where and how He can be adored.

"Then the king will say to those on his right hand, 'You have my Father's blessing; come, enter and possess the kingdom that has been ready for you since the world was made. For when I was hungry, you gave me food; when thirsty, you gave me drink; when I was a stranger you took me into your home, when naked you clothed me; when I was ill you came to my help, when in prison you visited me.' Then the righteous will reply, 'Lord, when was it that we saw you hungry and fed you, or thirsty and gave you drink, a stranger and took you home, or naked and clothed you? When did we see you ill or in prison, and come to visit you?' And the king will answer, 'I tell you this: anything you did for one of my brothers here, however humble, you did for me'" (Matthew 25:34-40).

What could be stated any plainer than that? How can we possibly misunderstand now? Suddenly, we can begin to see. We started this Experiment attempting to realize how much Jesus cares for us, all of us. And here He is saying again, in no uncertain terms, "Whenever there are people with needs, burdens, or trials, I am there. I walk the ways of life with you, my beloved little children. Are you looking for me?

"Remember this always. I am right here beside you in your greatest need. Because I am the Father, the Son, the Holy Spirit, I am able to be present also in the lives of people you meet. Is it hard for you to understand that I am the Ever-Present Christ?

Can you not accept this greatest of gifts, my Holy Spirit? It will make all the difference in life and in death if you will only become aware of this Presence within you and others.

"Listen to me. I suffer with your brother who is hungry and thirsty, for I am his Christ too. When you see his need and respond with love, you answer the greatest desire of my heart. You give food and drink to me. Be mindful that his hunger can be caused by more than lack of bodily nourishment; it can come from a starved mind, a thirsty deprived soul. I feel his need, for he is my child just as you are.

"I ache with loneliness, too, as I walk the stranger's way. I feel the cold winds of isolation, the terrible heat of prejudice, the dreadful storms of misunderstanding as my children suffer the indignities and injustice of the world. You can help to bear these burdens that weigh down upon their shoulders. They are my burdens too.

"I promise to be with you. Can't you believe me? Look for me in sickness of the body, in the trials of the mind and spirit, for I am there. Be as certain that I abide with you in these things you have to bear as you are that I am ever-present in the sufferings of all men. Do you want to help my pain, do you seek to unchain my fetters? I am waiting with your brothers for you to show that you care.

"O my child, I offer you the Ever-Present Christ. Beginning now, lasting forever, you can possess an awareness of my constant love. It is greater than all bounds of human conception, for it engulfs you in the stream of my eternal plan. Become aware of me as your Constant Counselor, and I will reveal myself to you. You will see me in every man you love."

EXPERIMENT—STAGE TEN

OBJECTIVE: For us to determine.

CONCLUSION: The Experiment has really just begun.